RECORDED LIVE

14.ii.70

RECORDED LIVE

★

New Pocket Cartoons

by

OSBERT LANCASTER

JOHN MURRAY, LONDON
1970

Osbert Lancaster's other works

Pocket Cartoons

Grateful acknowledgement is made to the Editor for
kind permission to reprint the drawings which
have appeared in the *Daily Express*

*Printed in Great Britain by Butler & Tanner Ltd., Frome a.
London, and published by John Murray, Albemarle Street, Lond*
0 7195 2067 3

FOREWORD

This present collection may, perhaps, be judged to be already of historical rather than topical interest. Since it was compiled June the 18th, the Night of the Crystal Balls, has come and gone. The world's great age begins anew, and our hearts are lifted up by the sight of fresh young faces aglow with a new enthusiasm and gladdened by the almost obtrusive evidence of a restored idealism. (Did I hear someone murmuring something about "women and champagne and bridge"? Perish the thought!)

Luckily, however, at least from the cartoonist's point of view, it seems likely that this regenerative process will be confined to the political scene. Elsewhere many of the old familiar figures, it may safely be assumed, will still be poised in their accustomed attitudes, their hair unruffled by the wind of change. Protesting students will continue to vindicate their democratic right to smoke pot; developers (and civil servants) will persist in desecrating the urban scene by the erection of unwanted office-blocks and the countryside with unnecessary air-fields; and assuredly some South Bank bishop will shortly be telling us that "O Calcutta" is a meaningful expression of contemporary religious awareness.

For us, therefore, it is all too clear that the time is not yet ripe for the abandonment of mental strife nor can our pencil sharpeners as yet sleep in our hands.

O. L.

July 1970

"Ulster will fight and Ulster will be right!" 20.vi.68

"Now suppose we drop the term 'overdraft' altogether and start talking about a new facility for sterling?" 10.vii.68

"But, Daddy, I don't *want* a vote—I want barricades!" 18.vii.68

"Speaking of sterilisation, how about the Sistine choir?" 1.viii.68

17.ix.68

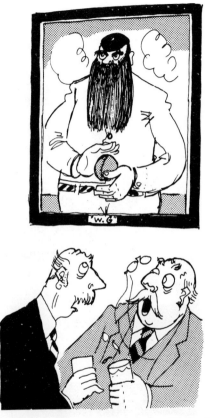

"May God forgive me, but just recently I've occasionally caught myself wondering exactly what colour he was underneath." 19.ix.68

"So don't risk damaging your vital organs by cigarette smoking—*we want them*!" 25.ix.68

"The Holy Father's quite right—it doesn't work!" 8.x.68

"Please might I borrow one just for half an hour, purely for demonstration purposes?" 16.x.68

"If the Belsize Park Young Trotskyites' Ad-Hoc Action Committee can't settle their differences in a spirit of fraternal co-operation Mummy's going to leave them behind." 26.x.68

"Vive la France! Vive le Général! Vive la gloire!
—And don't forget to buy me as many Deutsch-
marks as you can lay your hands on before the
market closes." 19.xi.68

"But of course they're going to have to legalise pot
—otherwise they can't tax it." 28.xi.68

"I can't help wondering, Miss Withit, if we are not perhaps in some danger of overstressing the contemporary aspect of the Christmas message."

13.xii.68

"Only one double-entendre in the whole dam'
show!" 18.xii.68

"Brahms has a very powerful message for Mildred." 20.xii.68

"But some of my best friends are Asians!" 10.i.69

"Circling the moon's all very fine, but those clever Russians are already having intercourse in outer space." 16.i.69

"Because if we were to launch a spaceship right now it's ten to one it would run aground on the Post Office Tower three minutes after blast off— that's why!" 17.i.69

"For Heaven's sake make up your mind and be quick about it—tomorrow's Sunday." 18.i.69

"Après nous le déluge! And it's up to us, mon
général, to see that it stays après." 30.i.69

"Honestly, darling, I'm not trying to rush you, but all my spies tell me it's not going to stay tax-free much longer." 5.ii.69

"Trust Aunt Ethel to make difficulties! She says she doesn't mind what we take her to on her birthday provided it's heterosexual and has a happy ending." 27.iii.69

"If only your family had concentrated a little more on genes and a little less on dowries you might have been way above the Snow-line by now."
12.iv.69

"Of course, you do realise, don't you, dears, that
were I to fall victim to involuntary euthanasia at
any time during the next seven years you'd be
liable for death duties at the standard rate?"
30.iv.69

"Well, actually, we're stifling our burning resentment of social injustice until the tele-cameras come along." 2.v.69

"Excuse me!" 22.v.69

"If you're so jolly sure that life is finally extinct, just try clearing away that glass and see what happens!" 4.vi.69

"I suppose you realise that we've also achieved
freedom from cash?" 11.vi.69

"Some women will put absolutely *anything* on their heads so long as it attracts attention."
18.vi.69

"You've nothing to lose but your chains!" 25.vi.69

"That's St Paul's, that was!" 24.vii.69

"But, Mummy darling, I don't want to become a witch—I've set my heart on going to London and becoming a traffic-warden." 31.vii.69

"Shaming as it may be, my dear, I feel I must point out that you yourself were successfully conceived by a couple of ignorant amateurs."

27.ix.69

"Now before we go any further, could we, please, get it quite clear which side of the fence we are, individually, on?" 15.x.69

"Gentlemen, let us get our priorities right! Historic buildings must not be allowed to stand in the way of expensive accommodation for the tourists who come to see these historic buildings." 17.x.69

"I was just saying how odd it is that one can freely spend £11,000 on a topless Italian sports-car but not a penny more than £50 on a visit to Florence."
22.x.69

1

"Has it not occurred to you, madam, that were I to dispose of it in the way you suggest I might easily do myself a grave physical injury?"
24.x.69

"Come along, children! Time for sex!" 28.x.69

"How typical! Too little, too late!" 31.x.69

"Oh no, we never have bomb outrages over here
—our sky-flats fall down quite by themselves."
14.xi.69

"Aldwych only!" 2.xii.69

"Not to worry! Spiro Agnew knew my father ..."
11.xii.69

"It's their trendier-than-thou attitude that I can't stand." 16.xii.69

"Let me warn you, dearly beloved, that, no matter what Convocation recommends, there'll be no skipping the 'miserable sinners' in this church."
15.i.70

"You remember that bomber we sold to the French for undercover resale to the Saudi Arabians for transfer to Biafra? Well, it got diverted to Israel and now it's been hijacked by Bernadette Devlin acting on behalf of the Welsh Nationalists." 17.i.70

The statue label reads:

NYMPH
AND
SATYR
FRENCH
17ᵗʰ CENT

"Still working for their O-levels, if you ask me."
6.ii.70

"O, doctor! Poor, darling Willy made it such fun that I'm very much afraid he's dislocated his hip!"
11.ii.70

"Mountbatten's right! One wouldn't so much mind
the thought of Denis Healey's finger on the
button if only one could be reasonably certain
that the Pentagon's thumb weren't on Denis
Healey." 25.ii.70

" 'Gooseflesh, J. Balliol. IQ, low. Physique, poor. Suffers from acne.' And not a word about my being a fully paid up member of the South Mimms Branch of the Young Trotskyist Association!"

28.ii.70

"Here beginneth the Tenth Chapter of the Book of
the Prophet Isaiah starting at the twelfth verse—
trad version." 17.iii.70

"Watch your step! Since he went on that refresher course on sex he's been asking some very tricky questions." 20.iii.70

"Any minute now Mr Wilson is going to call Mr Heath a smelly little squirt, and Mr Heath, quick as a flash, is going to tell Mr Wilson he's another."

25.iv.70

"The General has just been explaining that what might seem like intervention to old neo-colonialists such as ourselves is, in fact, all part of a policy of graduated de-escalation." 2.v.70

"Why on earth can't Ted Heath do something constructive—like having his aged grandmother kidnapped?" 7.v.70

"I'm afraid Great Aunt Ethel is in something of a quandary—she's rather keen on apartheid but is terribly anti-cricket." 19.v.70

"Who are you to flout the People's Will as democratically expressed in our infallible opinion polls?" 20.v.70

"We must thank our lucky stars, Ethel, that the Boers never took up croquet!" 22.v.70

"So I said to the polls fella you can put me down as an under twenty-five who thinks Harold Wilson's doin' a splendid job—and d'you know he did!" 6.vi.70